They Say I Missed My Calling

Kerry R. Jeffrey

In Dedication To:

I have made it a goal to dedicate every book that I write. I am writing this to simply dedicate it to a friend of mine; a brother of mine. Ever since we met, we've had this brotherly connection. He was a big supporter of my abilities with comedy being the biggest interest. Truly, he is one of those great people that made this book a reality. One day, I hope he gets to see an on-stage performance of my comedy just like we always planned.

So, here's to Ken Barnhill. Here's to my brother from another mother that I will always treat as my own blood.

And

Just

When

You

Thought

There

Would

Be

A

Content

Page

Nope. Sorry. Not in a comedy book. You're just going to have to survive. You'll just have to keep reading all the while not knowing what part you left off on for when you come back later trying to remember what page the joke was on. It's so very evil, I know. Ha ha! I mean, go buy a bookmark!

No really, I hope you enjoy this. I sure did.

Introduction

So, the consistency of how many times I have been told that I should have been a comedian was undoubtedly at a high count at this point. My superpower of quick wit and sarcasm has taken me this far so, why not put it all on paper.

It has been quite some time since the thought had first entered my head, but now is the time. A time that all this comedy, that I have written down, for it seems like years, comes to light in this book. That's right my friend! A book chopped full of my insane ramblings. You bet'cha!

Throughout the years, I have kept post-it notes, journals, composition notebooks, and even memos in my phone. It's time to put this down in a book so I can share with you, what my friends and family had always said, was hilarious. Enjoy.

Chapter One

Randomness

I love the word "random." It produces this value of shock and awe that I love. Let's face it, the unexpectedness in any comedy situation makes for some good laughs. I wanted this comedy book to be different because I am different. So, I am including anything and everything I have found funny over the years. This includes little quips, snarky comments, funny stories, and the random funny stuff I have found funny.

My first book, as far as comedy goes, was going to be one of those "Idiot" or "Do It Yourself for Dummy" type books. I think it would have sold well due to its value just as a gag gift alone. I was going to call it "Wipe Your Ass for Dummies." The first and only written page in the book was going to be some comical instructions on how to indeed wipe properly. That was funny enough on its own, but then I was going to make the following pages actual toilet paper sheets that you could tear out to use. I mean the value of this book increases by the number of men you know in your life that would need it.

Think about it, it'd be a great stocking stuffer for all those weird people you know. Think of all the campers, hikers, bikers, hunters, and truckers that would love this damn thing.

Okay, I promised randomness. Here we go:

I found out the hard way that the congratulatory butt smack you'd give in other sports is one you shouldn't give to a cyclist while you are hanging out the car window going 55 mph as you drive by them. It's a good way to make them hit the ditch though.

One night, I had a "come to Jesus" moment with a piece of string late one night. I hurriedly rushed into the bathroom and the wind from the door made a piece string scurry across the floor. I jumped away from it and yelled, "Jesus Christ!" It scared me so bad that it almost took care of the urination situation at the time. I am afraid of spiders, and, by God, it could have been one.

I wonder if the guy who announces the start of the wrestling matches ever used his voice in the bedroom. Like, "Let's get ready to sheet wrestle!!! R-r-ready to sheet wrestle!!!" It makes me wonder. On the same thought, the Big Bopper very well could have stood in the delivery room and sang, "Oooooohhhh Baby, I know that light is bright". What a way for his child to enter the world.

The definition of the time it takes to pick a wedgie out in public is now referred to as "One Cotton Picking Minute".

I always try to save myself a lot of embarrassment most of the time. I found out pretty quickly that doing the moonwalk is the only way to look cool while wiping dog crap off the bottom your shoes.

I do make it a point to hardly ever dress up really nice. It tends to get me into trouble. I just wanted to mention it. The last time I wore a tuxedo I had to live a long five years with a very grumpy woman.

Technology is certainly improving over the years. I still haven't seen a car that runs on trash though. Even better, they could make a car run off of just feces. It would prove to be a little more gross, but still, a more effective way of improving transportation. The only downfall would be the fact that no one would ever give a shit to see it run.

I still want to get a huge check and about fifty blown-up balloons. It'd be fun just to videotape someone walking up to a random person's door and make them think they won a lot of money. They would be handed the balloons and when they ask what they won, we'd say "A crap load of balloons!" Then we'd run away in the particular manner that Phoebe did on "F.R.I.E.N.D.S." laughing all the way.

I don't fully remember the dreams I dream but I do remember dreaming one night that I was the only dog on Noah's ark. Somehow, I ended up with both fleas. The last thing I remember was me looking up at Noah and mumbling, "That bitch!"

I often wondered if lizards know when they lose their tails. I imagine they go back to their tiny lizard dens and step halfway into the hole and say "Honey, you aren't going to believe this. I completely lost my freaking ass tonight." And she's like, "What...You did what? I told you to stop playing poker with the snakes!" Then he steps into the light, and she sighs saying, "Freaking hell Greg, I thought you meant something else. It'll grow back!"

If someone gets heartburn from eating a ton of weed brownies, you think that would be considered "chronic indigestion"?

McDonald's had a billboard near my house awhile back that read "Show your Dollar a Good Time". I mean, when did McDonald's start offering a McLap Dance?

Every time an attractive woman jump out of a huge cake, a fat guy dies just a little bit inside. That joke is multi-layered...just as the cake was.

Seeing photos of yourself as a child at a birthday party or a park is a lot like seeing drunk photos of yourself now. You don't really remember it and you aren't quite sure who all those other people are, but by all means, at least you look like you were having a great time.

I have a little picture that a carry around in my back pocket. It's of a midget dressed up like a leprechaun pimp with several women around him. Why do I have this picture? When I meet someone new, I reach for my pocket while asking them if they want to see a "Little Magic Trick".

Chapter Two

Because I Can

With me being somewhat of a bulky individual for the greater percentage of my life so far, I think I am well qualified to make a few fat jokes here and there. I am comfortable making these jokes so no one should feel bad for me while reading this chapter. So, let's raise our glasses, candy bars, or whatever you may have readily available, to this chapter. Let's give a toast to the chubbiest of our kind.

I hate watching commercials. If they had more "real" people in them then I might be more inclined to pay attention. Take for instance, the old Taco Bell commercial awhile back that claimed that their .99¢ menu would fill you up. My point being is, if they would've had a fat guy yelling "I'm full" in that commercial, Taco Bell would have gotten a lot of freaking money out of me. I might have even bought stock at that point. My thought would've been, "If they filled that big boy up, then I gotta go eat there". It's that simple.

Even when I was skinnier, I was more attracted to fuller figured women. I was one of those chubby chasers. Even though, I don't think it's correct to call someone that any longer. I was more of a chubby catcher. I make that comment in good stride because I hate to run. Running and fat don't mix too well. I have had dreams where I was running and woke up for lack of breath. But, I like chubby women. I like them so well that my friends started calling me Bounty because I was truly the quicker, thicker, picker-upper.

I remember when I was in the Marines, a few buddies and I got together to have a cook-out. My buddy was manning the grill when I heard him yell over at me saying, "Hey man, you want a fat patty or no?" I yelled back, "I don't know man. How old is she? She hot?" Needless to say, he spit his beer across the patio.

I always choose my potential relationships by weight. I always chose the girls that were around-about my same build. I never wanted to look in a mirror with one of us being skinner than the other, making us resemble the number ten. It's purely fractional on my part.

Being big does has its disadvantages. Shopping for clothes is a force to be reckoned with. Don't get me wrong, they have a lot of big and tall stores, but you never ever see any short and fat stores.

And it's becoming harder and harder to think of creative Halloween costumes when the original character is skinny. I always have to have a back story as to the reason why the character is fat now. I went as Shaggy Rogers from Scooby Doo one year. Apparently, I had to say that over the years, Shaggy gained some weight due to having too many munchies after he smoked out.

I have a love/hate relationship with my bathroom scale. Now, the maker of this particular scale's name is Health-O-Meter. I, on the other hand, see it differently and refer to it as a Fat-O-Dometer. It's the fastest thing I have ever seen. I step on it, and it goes from zero to two hundred in about two seconds.

Alright, that about covers it. There is so much more to write. Time to move on. That and I keep repeating the Bounty jingle in my head.

Chapter Three

Right Back at You

Often, I find myself in situations where I must think fast. It happens more often than normal to say the least. But it does keep me on my toes. I'll give you a few examples.

When I was stationed at Camp Pendleton in California for the Marine Corps, we had some time off, so we all traveled to see some of the state. Me and a group of buddies ended up at a mall in San Marino. We were there for hours. Within the time we were there, we kept running into this beautiful, redheaded girl and her entourage of friends. We just thought it was funny that everywhere we were; they were too. At one point, we all started laughing at something her friends did. They took notice of our laughter and before we knew it, she was walking towards us. With a snobbish attitude she asks us, "Ummm...what do you guys think you are laughing at?" Without missing a beat, I pushed myself to the front of the group and said, "Well it was someone we thought was beautiful until you opened your damn mouth." Her jaw dropped and we walked away.

Sometimes I like to be facetious, but only if it's done in a comedic way. With that being said, I'll tell you some delightful little stories.

I ran into a guy that was taking a call in a public restroom. Not only was he on the phone but it was on speaker, and it sounded as if it was a conference call. Now, I know that if people are in a pinch and have no other option, they'll do desperate things. Apparently, the conference call had already begun and that's when he hurried into the restroom. So, here I was, standing there washing my hands while trying to be as quiet as I could so to be courteous to this guy and not embarrass him. He hasn't even acknowledged that I am there and hasn't even looked up to see who I am. Upon leaving, I get this wild idea that I should make my presence known. Before I left, I yelled back into the room as the door closed, "Oh my God! New urinal pads!" Too bad that guy never knew what I looked like.

I forgot where I was, but I remember that this little Hispanic girl was talking to another little girl about how chubby I was. She kept running past me saying things like, "There's a fat fatty. See, I told you. A fatty fat-fat." Then she ran off to where her older sister or cousin was. I went up to her and made sure her guardian at the time could hear me and told her, "Hey, tell your parents that I wish them luck when you end up pregnant at fifteen." So, I left the area laughing. This left the older girl shocked and really confused, wondering why all this took place.

I hate it when people make fun of other people just to be a bully and make them appear better than they are. It's hurtful. This is where I tend to take up for the one being made fun of. I know what it's like and if given the chance to make the bully look bad, it's a guarantee that I am going to say something.

I once worked at a college. Occasionally, you would overhear things you may or may not want to hear. I walked past the fountain in the main atrium area when suddenly I heard a girl yell out to another girl that was walking down the hall. She cupped her hand and said, "Blue jean skirts are so 2001! Hello, out of style!"

Apparently, she was trying to make her two friends laugh with her. Too bad I heard what she said and replied with, "So, are sweater vest. What are you, forty?" I kept walking, she was shocked, and her friends laughed at her instead.

So, there you go, a well-deserved chapter about getting back at others and being comical at the same time.

Chapter Four

I Just Want To Throw This Out There

And here we are with another kind of random chapter. It's different because at one time this stuff has either happened to me, was told stories about someone I knew, or I opened my mouth at the wrong time. Seemed to be a pattern with me through life.

I think the outside packaging of edible underwear should have a warning that states not to wear them for an extended period of time. They stain!!!

I think if you are questioning whether or not you dropped a piece of chocolate between your legs, you should always double check. It'll save you from walking into a nice restaurant with what appears to be, soiled pants. It looked like I hit a deer!

I think you should never abbreviate the words Senior Technology Developer when calling it over the PA system to call one into a meeting room.

I think when you are asked what method you use when typing on a keyboard you should choose your words a little more carefully. Anything is better than telling the interviewer that you peck at the keys by calling yourself (and I quote) "A huge pecker."

I think small bladders utterly destroyed the button fly jeans industry. Therefore, I never bought another pair.

I think nuns and priests, in comparison to animals, are the neutered and spayed individuals of the human world.

I think the perfect redneck name for a little boy is, in fact, Holden O'Bier. Spoiler Alert...There is a person with this name.

I think the greatest tattoo idea that I have recommended someone get is one located on her mid-section being a sign in a patch of grass that reads "Keep off the Median".

I think if you listen to Usher's song, "Yeah!" when Lil' Jon says, "Yeah...What...Okay", I think you can easily replace him with Scooby Doo saying the exact same thing, and the song is still just as good.

I don't think it's wise to make a perverted joke out of the question, "Are you craving wood?" when a person has asked it of your pregnant wife at the WIC office.

I think imitation bacon is rightfully the prostitute of foods. Sure, most of the time it goes down the same, but you will most likely be up late that night paying for something that has left a bad taste in your mouth.

I think that if there was a test for the job of being a prostitute the oral and the practical would be the same thing.

I think that when you are talking about a vasectomy you should refrain from making a joke about a penis gun that shoots blanks.

I think the only reason that Emeril Lagasse's wife would ever complain about his love making ability is that he used too much essence and not enough BAM!

I think when you have the urge to party and you are too poor to buy shot glasses; votive candle holders work just as well.

I think all fire drills will always be a type of premature evacuation.

I think X has marked the spot for long enough. I think it's time V had some time in the spotlight.

I think Snoop Dogg could very well be considered the Willie Nelson of rap.

I think the economy has gotten so bad that no one can get dirty deeds done dirt cheap anymore.

I think it's funny when I think of the words "Sexually Transmitted Disease". It is abbreviated STD. But then on insurance paperwork, so is "Short Term Disability".
So really, depending on what disease you have, STD could rightly be considered a type of STD.

I think if I ever had a business, it'd be a lot like Hot Topic. I'd sell a lot of stuff that I personally would never buy for myself. I'd name the store something like "Anger". That's an appropriate name. When it came to hiring for the store, I would look forward to the hiring of store managers.
It's really just for the simple fact of saying, "So, why

do you believe you are the right person for Anger management?"

And last but not least... I don't think I would ever be able to own a dog called a chiweenie. I just don't want a dog that sounds like it belongs in Chinese porn.

And on that note,...I think... that's a wrap for this chapter.

Chapter Five

A Course in Perversion
(Like I haven't said anything before this chapter...)

Of course, we can't forget how funny a little bit of off-beat humor actually is.

It all started with one thing. Way back in the day, a woman by the name of Eve bit an apple and magically we are all aware that something is just not right. I still think it's funny that it was a little snake that started it all. Yet, if Eve never took a bite of the forbidden fruit, we would never have to ask stupid questions. We'd just know. A few questions come to mind, like:

"Honey, are you cold?"

"So, you think she's pretty?"

We used to take this intelligence test back when I worked for a retail store. I had no idea why it was named this, but it was, and it made us laugh every time we mentioned it. It was called the Wonderlic test. Now, Wonderlic sounds like a lesbian superhero to me. She carries her staff of confusion detailed with a tongue at the top of it. She's super strong unlike the other women superheroes. Maybe, she's like a Timex watch and takes a licking but keeps on ticking.

I figure at some point someone is going to question the fact of how the invisible man had sex. I don't know why, I just wonder about these things. I bet it was frustrating because no one ever saw him coming.

I have always questioned a fair number of things. I feel I must, or I would never come up with anything funny. I like catching people off guard as well.

My brother was driving a handful of us somewhere one time so, out of the blue, I thought I would break the silence. On most roads there are little bumps on the divider lines between the lanes. So, the problem was that he kept swerving into the other lane. I looked over at him and asked if by chance if he was a breast man. He says, "Yeah, why?" I quickly reply with, "I was just wondering because you are hitting those road nipples pretty hard."

Speaking of which, if you were blind and had to read everything in Braille, wouldn't nipples be epic?

Being a virgin is a lot like gambling. Sure, you're thinking you've got a good hand most the time, and you can always try your luck at the playing the slots but think about it this way. By the end of the night, you didn't find the cherries you thought you would, you're alone and broke, but you have the excessive need to do it all again tomorrow.

Morning sex is like an awkward, kinky version of Twister. All you're really trying to do is get as close as possible to someone or into as many different positions as possible without actually breathing on each other.

I have a unisex name, which is cool. I also always thought it'd be cool that I could be with someone with the same name as me, and when someone screams their own name during sex, no one would find it weird.

There's an old saying that goes: "Why don't you guys go belly up to the bar?" I think it's only fair that women can equally: "Boobie up to the bar."

Which if you think about it, they have done that for years just to get free drinks. So really, we all win.

The phrase, "Work smarter not harder" applies to everything except the adult film industry.

If you think about it, bungee jumping and prostitution have a lot in common. They pretty much cost the same, lasts just as long and if the protection breaks, you're screwed.

Did you know that scientists have found there is a line between love and hate? It's labeled with the abbreviation S.T.D.

Also, do you know that on a medical questionnaire for a pregnant woman to fill out before her appointment the "Withdraw Method" is labeled Coitus Interruptus? What in the name of Harry Potter's world are they trying to say?

There's a dish that's easy to make. It's a mixture of peas and corn. The mixture has been rightly named Porn. I get it. It's the combo of them both. But, not to worry, I would only eat it for the articles.

It's been said that a male has two brains but not enough blood to run both at the same time. That could be true. I like to think of it as having enough blood to run them both but sometimes it's difficult to keep the dirty thinking mind from whispering nasty shit in the other one's ear.

Thongs are like glass houses. They are pretty and they allow you to see a lot of things. The only issue is that it only takes one little crack to mess the whole damn thing up.

Condoms should come in different packages too. Why can't they be packaged like Band-Aids are? They usually come with cartoons or at least something of interest on them. Trust me, I have put some thought into this. If condoms came in a variety three pack with a Big Bird (feathered for her pleasure), an Elmo (tickling sensation), and a Snuffleupagus(for those longer in the trunk), it would be awesome! And another one that could be considered is The Flintstones. The titles for those could be Bedrock Cock, Bam-Bam Thank you Ma'am, and the Yabba Dabba Do Me. We could have ones named after movies. Ones like The Big Lebowski, Big Trouble in Little China, and Reservoir Dogs. And the ones that made me laugh the most: Police officer condoms with names like The Billy Club, The Night Stick, and The K-9 Unit.

Chapter Six

Too Much Time On My Hands

Along with being random, I am creative. I like to create things that are entertaining to read. I think I got it from watching late night television. I used to love when David Letterman had list and when Johnny Carson had monologues. So, I have created a few things and made-up funny stories that I feel were laughable yet entertaining.

True Story-

I went to the mall one morning to shop for new pants. This was before I got chunky and didn't need Short and Fat stores. I walk past the entry doors right beside where I checked out and this woman goes running out after this other woman. I looked at what was going on and then heard this woman yell very loudly into her walkie talkie, "Security to lingerie! We have a snatch and grab. We have a runner in lingerie!"
So...I help get the license plate of said runner and everyone calms down, they say thank you, and I was on my way.

I'd been driving for a minute or so when it occurred to me that someone had yelled very loudly into a device in which everyone else could hear over the intercom about a snatch and grab with a runner in lingerie.

Today in "Fake News", a local event planner accidentally scheduled two groups on the same day at the convention center. Aaron's, a local furniture rental and delivery store's goodtime shindig was interrupted by the People with Tremors Support Group meeting.
In related news, everything worked out at the convention center when both got together and are planning an event next year aptly named "The Movers and Shakers Ball".

Ok...
So I choose not to know a lot about the undead. I have never watched The Walking Dead or anything. I mean, I did enjoy the Resident Evil movies, but I digress.
Oh..okay so,... I feel something must be addressed. Zombies are dead but still alive doing living things, right? I mean, they still must eat. You only eat to stay alive right? Why does the "sort of" dead still

need to eat? For that matter, do they still have to use the bathroom too? The substantial nutrients must go somewhere...

And if they attack you and end up eating your brain does that make you dead "dead" or are you just a vegetable zombie? If they eat your brain, get sick from your living head, and end with a stomachache from it, do they then poop "your" brains out?

There was mass confusion years ago when several small children were believed to be lost inside Disney World. One was believed to be trapped inside the Small World ride. Officials were confused to whether it was a boy or girl at the time. The child was finally retrieved by a grounds man in which upon the retrieval he began to sing, "It's a small girl after all...."
It was pretty much a sing-along after that for at least five minutes.

And now for the list portion...

If cuss words were abbreviated, they would stand for these...

Shit- Stupidly Heading Into Turmoil
Fuck- Fornicating Unknowingly Causing Kids
Damn- Damaging All Men's Namesake
Cunt- Clearly Used Notable Trash
Hell- Hope Everyone Loves Lucifer
Bitch- Beastly Individuals That Cause Havoc
Piss- Purposely Ignoring Sanitized Standards

Now I present to you "15 Things You Can Say In A Mechanic Shop That You May Or May Not Say In The Bedroom".

1. Can you back it some so I can get a better angle?
2. Turn it to the left a little bit so I get my eyes on it.
3. Oh, hell! I stripped it.
4. Try pumping it three times before you start it up again.
5. I can get under there; I just don't have any breathing/elbow room.
6. I'm gonna need a bigger tool to loosen that up.
7. Looks like your back end needs realignment.
8. I just need to top you off, and you'll be good to go.
9. When was the last time you got it serviced?
10. I can see it. I just can't get my hands on it.
11. You might want to think about getting your

headlights adjusted.

12. Front and back look good! You can go and switch the lights off.

13. The body is great, but what happened to the grill?

14. Has your undercarriage suffered any kind of impact?

15. We may have to lubricate it until it starts moving.

I call this next selection "Geek Speak Sexy Lingo". All my nerds will appreciate this.

RAM- Repeatedly Administrating Masturbation

Floppy- What happens a short time after RAM

Hard Drive- Thrusting when you are way too excited

External Hard Drive- She has toys

Scanner- Look her over. Tell her what you like

Virus Scan- No STD checklist

Megabyte- More than a little nibble

Gigahertz- Pain associated with Megabyte

Buffering- What's left after the condom breaks

Trojan- History tells us that a sneak attack through the back door

Phishing- Trying to find the condom

Spyware- Sneaking a peek

Raw File- Just give yourself some time to heal

Cold Start- Not tonight Honey

Phreaking- *I think that one is pretty clear

Thanks for reading. I'll be honest, I've really enjoyed this. I hope you have too. May you share this book and I hope maybe it becomes the staple of every one of your bathroom mainstays as far as reading material.

#comedybookgoals

www.ingramcontent.com/pod-product-compliance
Lightning Source LLC
Chambersburg PA
CBHW060644030426
42337CB00018B/3445